Survival Family Basics

The Prepper's 'Lights Out' Guide to Surviving with the Grid Down

Macenzie Guiver

I0427854

Macenzie Guiver

© 2014

Printed in the United States of America

Just to say Thank You for Purchasing this Book I want to give you a gift 100% absolutely FREE

A Copy of My Upcoming Special Report "The Prepper's Supplies Guide for When Disaster Strikes"

Go to www.SurvivalFamilyBasics.com to Sign Up to Receive Your FREE Gift

Table of Contents

Introduction

I want to thank you and congratulate you for purchasing, *"Survival Family Basics - The Prepper's 'Lights Out' Guide to Surviving with the Grid Down"*.

Electric power is the foundation on which much of our modern world is built. From providing safe drinking water to heating our homes, electricity underpins almost everything we do. It has become essential to providing every necessity for human life and without it, many people will suffer and even die simply because they do not know how to live safe and healthy lives without it.

The possibility of a grid down situation is very real. Whether it is a terrorist group that attacks several substations or a burst of electromagnetic energy exploding from the sun, the electrical grid that provides the power we use to live our lives is vulnerable. Something as small as an operator error has the potential to plunge the entire country into darkness for a day, a week, or possibly indefinitely. Meanwhile, most people do not have the skills or the resources to live for more than a few days without power or support.

This is why I put this book together. Every family needs to understand the risks associated with our electrical grid so that they can plan and prepare themselves to manage in a world without power, whether it's for a week, a month, or indefinitely.

This book provides an in-depth view of what it will mean to the modern world when the grid goes down and offers practical suggestions for how to prepare now in order to be ready after.

From learning how to create potable water to considering how to heat your home without power, this book will get you thinking about how you will keep your family safe and healthy during a power outage so that you will be ready to handle the worst of what happens when the grid goes down.

Thanks again for purchasing this book. I hope you enjoy it!

Macenzie Guiver

What Happens When the Grid Goes Down

If the grid goes down for any extended period of time it will impact every area of our lives. Most of us no longer have the skills or equipment needed to take care of our families, feed our children, heat our homes, and survive for long periods of time without access to electricity. For many prepping families, planning for a long-term grid down scenario is one of the most significant prepping challenges they undertake because of how all-inclusive their planning must be.

Remember, grid down doesn't mean the same thing as losing power for a few hours or even a couple of days because of an accident or a storm, it means living in a world without power.

A World Without Power

The difference between a power outage and the grid going down is very simple, power outages are local or regional and a grid down scenario is national. If you have ever experienced a power outage that lasted for several days, you know how quickly things we normally take for granted can become a problem. To demonstrate what it means to live in a world without power, let's start with the immediate and short term impacts and paint a picture of the new world we will be living in.

Short Term Impacts – Days 1 and 2

Limited or No Access to Running Water
- If you get your water from a well, you won't have access to water beyond what is currently in your toilets, tanks, and pipes.

- If you have city or town water, you may or may not have access to water. This will be dependent on whether or not the water treatment and pumping facilities have backup power and if that backup system functions as expected. If you have water, you may need to boil it or use as little as possible to help keep from overloading the back-up system which will not provide the same capacity as the primary system.
- No water means no toilets, no showers, and no tap water coming from a sink or hose.

No Access to Lighting and Appliances

- You will no longer be able to use any heating or cooling source in your home that requires electricity which includes furnaces, water heaters, and air conditioning systems that run on gas, oil, or propane since most of them require electricity as well.
- You will not be able to use any electrical lighting in your home or office
- You won't be able to use any appliances or electronics like the stove, oven, toaster, washer, dryer, radio, television, etc.

Limited Access to Food

- You will have access to whatever non-perishable food items you have on hand but you may not have water or a heating source to cook with which may limit your options
- The food in your refrigerator will remain viable for 4-8 hours and the food in the freezer will only be good for 1-2 days
- Restaurants with backup power may be open for service but they will be few and far between

Limited Access to Commerce
- If you don't have cash, you won't be able to buy anything
- ATMs will not be able to dispense money
- Credit and debit cards will be useless
- Some gas stations may have back-up power and fuel to sell but many will not be able to pump the gas out of their underground tank in order to sell it
- Stores may close and remain closed, some will operate with limited back-up power but cash will be required to make any purchases
- Many businesses will close until the power is restored

Limited Access to Communications and Information
- Cell phone service may be available as many towers and carrier systems have backup power capabilities, but they may not be accessible because of the volume of traffic
- Landline phone service should remain available as these systems also have backup power but similar problems may be experienced in terms of line traffic
- Television and radio broadcasters may be able to continue broadcasting for a limited amount of time by operating on backup power but many people will not have electricity to see or hear the broadcasts
- Sporadic access to the internet via smart phones may continue for a short time but since many of the servers that house the content that makes up the internet will be offline, the usefulness of any limited access is unknown

Limited Access to Local Government, Services and Infrastructure
- Schools will close or be opened with backup power as emergency shelters

- Local government offices may close if they do not have backup power
- Emergency services like police, fire, and medical facilities will be operating on back-up power
- Nuclear power plants will remain online and switch to backup power for operation
- State and National government offices and departments will be operating on emergency power generators and back-up power sources
- Medical centers and military and national guard bases will also be operating on emergency back-up power

Limited Access to Transportation
- Traffic lights and street lights go dark, making it more dangerous to drive
- Subways and trains will stop on the tracks, stranding people in tunnels and along the route
- Taxis will continue to operate but will require cash up front and may charge additional fees
- Buses and ferries will continue to run as long as they have fuel unless this service is halted by local government
- Airports will be operating on emergency back-up power which will be limited to landing planes already in the air, departing flights will be cancelled
- Many people will not be able to return home

Other Challenges
- People will be trapped in elevators, on amusement park rides, in gondolas, and on ski lifts
- Electronic security systems will not be operational
- The stock market will shut down
- Electronic money transfer and access will be unavailable

For anyone who has every lived through a power outage, that list of immediate impacts may make it seem like I am overstating the case. Power outages happen all the time and people survive without power for hours, days, even weeks. But we only need to revisit history to see that the seriousness of this kind of wide-spread power outage cannot be overstated, even in the first two days.

In the blackout of 2003, more than 55 million people were without power for somewhere between a couple hours and a couple days. During that time, 11 people died, thousands were stranded in elevators, subway cars, airports, and on city streets, and there were more than 60 all-hands on fires in New York City alone. The majority of these fires were the direct result of the use of alternative lighting and cooking sources. Raw sewage was inadvertently dumped into the Cataraqui River in Ontario, Canada, there was an explosion at a Marathon Oil refinery near Detroit, and trucks backed up for miles in Canada unable to leave because they had no access to fuel. New York State emergency services responded to more than 80,000 calls, twice as many as normal. And this was a relatively short, albeit widespread, outage that only impacted portions of one region of the country.

In looking back at that event, which was the second largest power outage in the world at the time, the most important factor to understand is that the 2003 outage wasn't caused by any physical damage to the grid or its components; it was caused by a software bug in an alarm system at one of the power plants. This is why power was restored as quickly as it was in most of the affected areas. It would have been a very different story if the outage resulted from damage to the electrical grid like we saw in Hurricane Katrina and Super Storm Sandy.

What many of us do not realize is that small power outages immediately create new dangers and risks that the majority of us are not used to handling. If you consider that every power outage we have ever experienced has been a partial outage where parts of a city, sections of a state, or even a large region have lost power, it is easy to see how the massive implications of a grid down scenario can be difficult to grasp.

Unfortunately, by the time many people realize what is possible, it will be too late for them to do anything except react and try to survive.

One of the things that make major power outages like those experienced in 2003 and with Super Storm Sandy different from a grid down scenario is that during those outages there are unaffected areas from which supplies like food, water, and fuel could be brought into the affected area. If the grid goes down, there won't be unaffected areas to help because we will all be affected.

So, that's the first few days….but they are nothing compared to what is coming.

3 Days to 3 Weeks Without Power

Around the third day of a major power outage or grid down scenario, the back-up power solutions for most critical services will begin to fail as those locations run out of fuel. *No Access to Running Water, Very Limited Access to Water*

- Generally, by the third day, no matter where you live you will have no access to clean, potable running water
- As backup systems at water treatment plants and pumping stations fail, so will the tap and sewer.

- There is a significant risk of sewage backup or accidental release which means any water that is available should be considered not potable until treated
- Toilets everywhere will be unusable and a sanitation crisis will rapidly escalate
- Without access to toilets, people, especially those living in cities with limited access to feasible alternatives, will use whatever space they can find to urinate and defecate, which will further compromise the safety of any available water source.
- Any store with a supply of potable water will likely open but the price of that water will be exorbitant and only cash or barter will be accepted
- People will begin drinking from unsafe sources of water out of desperation and water-borne disease will spread

No Access to Light, Heat, Cooling
- Depending on the season, the inability to heat or cool homes will quickly create very dangerous situations.
- If it is winter, people will seek alternative ways to heat and light their homes. The use of candles, fireplaces, and outdoor grills to provide heat and light will cause fires and carbon monoxide poisoning.
- If it is summer and the conditions are hot and/or humid enough, people will become ill and even die from the heat. The extra exertion required for climbing stairs, walking to destinations, and searching for resources in the heat can quickly lead to heat exhaustion, especially for those lacking access to adequate water.

Limited or No Access to Food
- You will need to dispose of all the perishable food products in your fridge and freezer, especially if you

plan to remain in your home. These items are no longer safe to eat and failing to remove them can expose you and your family to food borne illness

- Cooking will become more challenging as you have used up the "easy" food from your kitchen and pantry and without a stove, oven, or microwave to use in food preparation, you may begin to run out of safe food to feed for your family.
- Restaurants that were able to remain open will run out of fuel for their backup generators and be forced to close
- Grocery store shelves will either be picked clean, looted, or the store owners will be charging incredibly high prices for whatever stock they have left
- Deliveries of food won't be made as fuel shortages essentially stop the movement of goods across the country
- National guard units may begin distributing emergency food and water supplies, but the amount available will be limited and quickly exhausted
- People will start to panic as the realization that there is very little food remaining and no guarantee of when more will arrive sets in
- Violence over access to food and other resources becomes more and more likely at this stage

Extremely Limited Access to Commerce

- Cash and barter will be the only accepted forms of currency
- Gas stations will run out of fuel to sell and fuel to run their operations
- Stores may remain open but limited supplies and super-high prices will make any goods that are available out of reach for most people

No Access to Communications or Information

- Cell phone service will become inaccessible as backup systems run out of fuel
- Landline phone will also become unavailable as the phone companies run out of fuel
- The ability to call 9-1-1 will be almost non-existent, making it more challenging to access emergency services
- Dissemination of information will become increasingly challenging as backup systems run out of fuel and television and radio stations go dark

Almost No Access Local Government, Services and Infrastructure

- Local government and infrastructure services that were operating on backup power will shut down as fuel supplies are exhausted
- Curfews are likely to be imposed to limit injuries and looting
- Emergency services like police and fire may still be operating on backup power but their fuel supplies for backup generators will be almost gone. Additionally, their ability to respond to calls will be impacted by the lack of fuel for their vehicles, the loss of 9-1-1 dispatching services, and the blockage of roads by abandoned vehicles
- State and National government offices and departments will be forced to operate without power as the fuel for their backup systems is exhausted
- Medical centers will begin losing patients as they run out of fuel for their generators, patient care will be compromised, and only rudimentary medical services will be available
- Military and National Guard bases will continue operating on emergency back-up power or without power.

- Soldiers and national guards men will be deployed around the country to enforce curfews, handle food and water dispersal, and mitigate any civil unrest
- Martial law may be established in certain parts of the country
- Nuclear power plants will continue to operate using backup power

Almost No Access to Transportation
- People will abandon their cars wherever they run out of gas, leaving roads and highways blocked with stopped cars
- Airports will close
- Taxis, buses, and ferries will run until their fuel supplies run out
- Many people will still not be able to return home

Other Challenges
- Civil unrest, looting, hoarding, and violence will be on the rise as the uncertainty of the situation causes good people to panic and less than good people to take advantage of the opportunity

It's not a pretty picture and certainly not a situation most people would want to find themselves in for 3 weeks or even 3 days. But the real issue with a grid down situation is that we would be lucky if the power outage lasted only three weeks because the projections from the experts paint a much grimmer picture.

Long Term Impacts

The long term impacts of the grid going down are dependent on what took it down in the first place. There are a variety of scenarios that could lead to the loss of the entire electrical grid, each of which carries different consequences and caveats about how long the power would be out and how bad things would really be before it was restored. To demonstrate, let's look at a few grid down scenarios generally considered to be the most likely to cause the grid to do down.

Physical Terrorist Attack

One of the reasons the power grid provides an excellent target for terrorists is that it is a complex system with many well recognized vulnerabilities that can easily be attacked with very little risk to the attacker. While it might seem as though taking down the entire country's grid would require taking out a large number of targets, a study conducted by the Federal Energy Regulatory Commission indicates that a single attack that took out 9 key substations out of the 55,000 that make up the grid could cause the entire grid to collapse, creating a national blackout that would last for months. Unfortunately, the sheer size and quantity of substations, transformers, lines, and power plants that make up the grid make it impractical and almost impossible to guard from a physical terror attack. Many of the most important components are located in remote locations that are not even monitored by people onsite. Disruptions at almost any point in the system could be enough to damage components, cause power surges, and overload the system until it collapses.

Some of the most vulnerable aspects of the grid are the high voltage transformers. Several factors make these integral parts of the system very difficult and time consuming to replace. If enough of them were knocked out in a single attack, it could take months or even years to obtain enough replacements to completely restore power.

The knowledge and information required to identify and locate the right choke points to inflict the most damage, plan a coordinated attack, and implement that plan are well within the capabilities of known terrorist groups.

Cyber Terrorist Attack

What may be even more frightening to consider is that a terrorist organization wouldn't even need to have people on the ground physically attacking the power grid components to thrust the entire country into darkness. All they need is a computer and the right plan of attack because the power grid is so susceptible to being taken down by cyber terrorism. The modern grid is heavily reliant on automation, high-speed communications, and the ability to monitor and control remote equipment from centralized locations. That means they are connected to computers that can talk to each other which is all you need for a hacker to launch a cyber attack. The most vulnerable part of the system is also the most important, called SCADA. This stands for the Supervisory Control and Data Acquisition systems that enable real-time monitoring, measuring, and communicating to happen across the disparate power plants, substations, transformers, and transmission lines that make up the grid.

With access to SCADA, hackers wouldn't even need to plant a virus or do anything drastic to cause catastrophic damage to the grid. They could simply manipulate SCADA to disrupt the flow of power, display false indicators and signals to operators, interrupt the flow of information that is used to manage the grid, and/or disable the measures that have been put in place to try and protect the grid from terrorist attacks or other catastrophic events.

Many experts feel that a cyber attack by itself isn't likely to be able to cause the kind of damage that would leave us in the dark for months. But, if this kind of attack was coordinated with an attack on physical assets, it could enhance the effectiveness of the physical attack and possibly do more damage to the hard-to-replace components than a physical attack could do alone.

Operator Error/Aging Infrastructure

The workforce that currently monitors, repairs, and upgrades the various components that make up the power grid is getting older and as the highly qualified, experienced engineers begin to retire, they will have to be replaced. However, there are concerns about whether or not there will be enough qualified people available to fill the number of positions that will be required to maintain adequate staffing levels. When you add this to the aging of the infrastructure on which the grid is built, it quickly becomes clear that we may not even need a terrorist attack to find ourselves in a prolonged blackout.

The transmission grid is old, out of date, and already under stress from the ever increasing demands of our automated, computerized, smart phone carrying country. The loss of key components, failure of one part of the system, or even operator error could cause catastrophic cascading damage and we would have no one to blame but ourselves. These two factors also make the grid more susceptible to attacks from external parties as inexperienced engineers and outdated equipment may prolong the process of getting the grid back up and power flowing.

EMP/Solar Flare

Another risk to the grid comes in the form of something called an EMP, electromagnetic pulse. An EMP is a wave of energy that has been shown to have a detrimental effect on electronics and that could be used to knock out the systems we use to control the flow of energy between regions and across the country.

The kind of damage an EMP could do depends on the size of the wave. Small EMPs can interfere with radio and television transmissions. A medium EMP can create a spark which can ignite things that are highly flammable like gasoline fumes. A large EMP can cause damage to electrical circuits and equipment by creating powerful currents and high voltage that streams through them, damaging components and rendering them inoperable. A very large EMP can cause physical damage to structures, trees, and even planes. An example of a very large, focused EMP is a lightning strike. EMPs can be produced by natural forces, like lightning, solar flares, and coronal mass ejections, and with man-made means, like nuclear weapons. There are two possible scenarios where an EMP could cause catastrophic damage to the grid.

The first would be a direct hit from a very powerful coronal mass ejection (CME). A CME is a huge shockwave of electromagnetic radiation that shoots out into space from the sun that causes a geomagnetic storm when it comes into contact with the Earth's atmosphere. These powerful shockwaves can knock out satellites, disrupt radio communications, and if powerful enough, damage electrical transmission lines and facilities causing the grid to go down. Depending on the size and force of the EMP created by a CME, it could affect anywhere from a single region to the entire country to the entire day side of the planet.

The second would be the detonation of a nuclear weapon about 250 miles above the Earth's surface over the United States. The explosion would produce an EMP powerful enough to take out the power grid without doing any of the other damage we associate with a nuclear bomb. A single detonation could knock out power from Chicago to New York for months. More than one detonation could take down the entire grid. Estimates to repair this kind of damage top $2 trillion dollars and could take 10 years.

Long Term Survival in a World Without Power

Now that we have a foundational understanding of what a world without power looks like in the short term and what kind of situations could take the grid down for the longer term, it's possible to start talking about how long "long term" might be. This is an important piece of the preparedness puzzle because living without power for 3 weeks or even 6 weeks is a much different scenario that living without power for 3 months or 3 years.

The truth is, we just don't know how long the power will stay out if the grid goes down. There are so many factors at play and so many things that can impact the duration of the outage that it is impossible to speculate without actual information related to a situation that is actually happening. Some of the factors that can play a role in determining how long the power remains out include:

- The amount and type of physical damage done to the components that makes up the grid. For example, if parts, like the custom-built transformers, are damaged it could take months and possibly even years to replace those parts.
- The number of substations, transformers, etc. that have been damaged. This matters because utility companies have built up a stockpile of replacement parts in an effort to minimize these risks but that stockpile is only so big. If enough components are damaged, there may not be enough replacement parts available to restore power.
- How extensive the damage is in terms of geographical area. Operators may be able to route the flow of power around damaged parts of the system in order to restore power to the majority of the country, but if

there are too many damaged parts or if critical
components are inoperable this may not be possible.

Water

In a grid down situation, one of the first things you need to address is access to water. On average, a person can only live for 3 to 5 days without water and while most Americans understand the difference between water that is safe to drink and water that is not, they don't have a comprehensive understanding of the details or the consequences. Water has to be the number one priority as it can take time and energy to find a source of water, collect and transport that water, and then make it safe to drink.

As previously outlined, whether or not you have access to potable, which means safe to drink, water in the immediate aftermath of a major power outage will depend on where your water comes from and how prepared you are.
If you have a well, you won't have access to the water from that well unless you have some alternative way of powering it. This may be a generator, solar or wind power, or a hand pump.

If you get your water from a water system, you may continue to have access to potable water for several days after the power goes out or your tap may stop flowing immediately. The determining factor here will be whether or not the town or city water system you are using has backup power in place to use during power outages. During the outage, you will need to monitor communications from the local government about the ongoing safety of the government-provided water supply. Even if backup systems are in place, history has shown us that this isn't always enough to protect the water supply.

Regardless of which situation applies to you, you will need to know how to find, store, and purify water in the event that your primary water source is unavailable for any reason.

Finding It

Even if you don't have access to your primary supply of running water, you have some potable water in your house that can be accessed in the immediate aftermath of a power outage. The water in the tanks of your toilets, not the bowls, just the tanks, is potable so long as you have not added any cleansers or chemicals to it. If you have a traditional hot water heater, the water in that tank is potable and it can be drained and used for drinking water.

Depending on where you live, you may have access to non-potable found water sources. The water found in lakes, streams, rivers, ponds, reservoirs, canals, and even swimming pools and can be collected and used for drinking water as long as it is filtered and purified first. You may also be able to harvest rainwater, depending on the season, which can be made potable by purifying as it doesn't generally need filtration first.

Storing It

In order to ensure you have a safe source of potable water adequate to meet the needs of your family during an extended power outage, your best bet is to store enough water now to meet your family's immediate and short term needs. This will give you the luxury of time to assess and address your longer term needs.

The main challenge with storing water is space. Water is heavy and it takes up a lot of room. Optimally, potable water should be stored inside away from sunlight. Potable water must be stored in clean, sterile containers that are suitable for this purpose. Any plastic container that ever held anything but food should not be used to store water. Additionally, only plastic containers that are constructed of food grade materials should be used for storing water.

In order to determine how much water you need to store in order to provide your family's needs in the short term, you need to consider the number of people, their gender, their age, any special requirements (like formula for infants), and your climate. Generally, men over 18 need 3.7 liters of water per day which is roughly a gallon of water and women over 18 need about 2.7 liters or ¾ of a gallon. You might notice this is more than the 64 ounces most people think you need. While children generally need less than this, plan to store the same ¾ gallon for each child which will give you a little buffer.

For a family of four, this means you need about 3.25 gallons of potable water for drinking per day. Storing 50 gallons of water would provide enough drinking water for about 15 days.

You also need to figure in the water you need for purposes other than drinking. Cooking, dishwashing, and hand washing also require potable water. In an ideal world, potable water would also be used for bathing and washing clothes but we have stepped outside of ideal at this point. To be safe and ensure you have enough water to meet your family's basic needs for drinking and basic hygiene, you should plan for an additional 6 to 12 liters, 1.5-3 gallons, per person.

This brings your total daily potable water requirements for a family of four to around 12- 15 gallons per day. Now, that 50 gallon drum of stored water will last you 3-4 days.

Purifying It

Even if you have a backup plan in place to provide potable water, and are storing water to use in the immediate aftermath of a power outage, you will, at some point, need to collect found water and make it potable. There are several methods for doing this, each requiring different supplies and resources. The more you know about how to create potable water and the more options you have available, the better able you will be to ensure you can meet the needs of your family.

Filtration

There are only three circumstances where you do not need to filter found water before purifying it. First, if you are using a commercial product that filters and purifies the water, you won't need to filter it separately. Second, if you are using harvested rainwater that has fallen from the sky into your container, it should be free of particulates requiring filtration. Third, if you are using the distillation method, filtration is not required.

If you do not have a commercial filter specifically designed to purify water in emergency situations, you can create one with materials that should be easy to find. Start with a large container and a piece of plastic tubing. Poke a hole near the bottom of the container that is just barely large enough to insert the tubing through. Secure the tubing and then add several inches of gravel to the container. Next add a thick layer of charcoal. This can be regular charcoal from a fire pit or wood stove or activated charcoal. While activated charcoal is better overall for filtering, it is not something you can make at home so unless you already have some on hand, regular charcoal will do the trick. Next, add a layer of sand. Each layer should take up a little more than ¼ of the container so that the material fills the container slightly more than ¾ full. Cover the container with a piece of fabric so that it is spread taut over the top and then pour the water in the top to filter it. Once it is filtered, it should still be disinfected using one of the methods outlined below.

Boiling
Boiling is the best way to make filtered water safe to drink as it will kill the majority of microorganisms that cause water-borne illnesses. Bring water to a boil and allow it to boil for at least one minute then cool before drinking.

Disinfection
Filtered water can also be rendered potable by disinfecting it with chemicals or ultraviolet light. The two most common chemicals used are household bleach and iodine. To disinfect water with household bleach, you will need to add 1/8 teaspoon of regular, non-scented household bleach for each gallon of water and then allow the water to sit for 30 minutes. To disinfect with iodine, add 20-40 drops of an iodine tincture that contains 2% iodine and 47% alcohol for each gallon of water and then allow the water to sit for 30 minutes. Disinfecting with ultraviolet light requires a specific tool that can be used to render filtered water biologically safe.

Distillation
Distillation uses heat and evaporation to create potable water from any water source. It takes time and the construction of a still in order to produce any quantity of water, but it will remove physical contaminants, biological contaminants, heavy metals, and most chemicals. This is the method that will yield the purest water. For distillation, you need to boil your found non-potable water so that you can collect the water vapor produced by evaporation. When this water vapor encounters a hard surface, it condenses back into water and that water is potable. The key is trapping the water vapor as it rises, allowing it to condense on a safe surface, and then capturing it.

You can create a simple still with a large stockpot with a lid, a small bowl, and some string. Tie the string around the bowl and attach it to the stockpot lid so that when you put the lid on the stockpot upside down, the bowl is suspended below it. Fill the stockpot half full of water and heat it on high heat. As the water boils, water vapor will rise and collect on the lid of the stockpot. Because the lid is inverted, the condensed water will run down the slope of the lid and into the bowl. The water in the bowl is distilled and safe to drink.

What to do now to be ready

1. If you have a well, have a backup plan in place for how you will power the well during a blackout.
2. If you have town/city water, find out if the water system has a backup system in place to power the system during an outage and how long those backups will be able to provide safe drinking water during an outage.
3. Find out how information about the safety of your drinking water will be communicated by the town, city, or water department during a power outage.
4. Locate local sources of water like streams and lakes so you know where they are when you need them.
5. Begin storing water to meet your family's immediate needs.
6. Invest in water filtration equipment that can be used to easily transform found water into potable water.
7. Add the supplies necessary for chemical disinfection and distillation to your list of preps so that you have as many options for creating potable water as possible.
8. Consider storing enough activated charcoal to build your own filter in the event of a long term outage.
9. Build a solar still and practice distilling water.

Hygiene

Hygiene and sanitation are two things most people don't put much thought into until the power goes out. Our unfettered access to a seemingly endless supply of safe drinking water has spoiled us to the point that many of us have no idea what to do when the water stops running and the toilet stops flushing.

This problem quickly became apparent in the wake of Hurricane Katrina when the plumbing system of the Superdome, which housed more 20,000 survivors for several days, failed. With no other options, survivors were forced to use clogged toilets until they were full and then to find other places to urinate and defecate which filled the space with the stench of raw sewage and opened the door to illnesses caused by unsanitary conditions.

Safe handling of human waste is crucial to the health and safety of your family.

Latrines

Your sanitation needs in the immediate aftermath of a power outage can likely be met with the toilet in your home. If you continue to get water from a well or a water system, you should also be able to use the toilet as usual. If you do not have running water, you may be able to use the toilet but you will need to add water to the tank or bowl in order to make the toilet flush. However, if the toilet stops working or becomes clogged and cannot be unclogged at any point, do not continue to use them! If there is human waste in the bowl when this happens, you need to clean it out and dispose of it properly. Never leave a clogged toilet full of excrement in your living environment and never use other bathroom facilities like sinks or bathtubs as toilets.

If you do not have access to a toilet or the toilet you have been using becomes clogged, you will need another option. The easiest short term option is to create a toilet using a 5 gallon bucket, a trash bag, some duct tape, and kitty litter. Use the trash bag to line the inside of the bucket and secure it with duct tape. Keep the bucket covered when not in use and add a scoop of kitty litter after each use to absorb liquids and help manage the smell. Dispose of the bag by tying the top into a knot and burying the bag at least 200 feet from any water source. For long term use, construct a traditional outhouse.

There are many different ways to build an outhouse; here are some of the basics you will need to design one that is right for you. While a traditional outhouse is relatively easy to construct, it does take a little time and some materials.

1. Choose your location. Most experts agree that it should be 100-200 feet from any water source. If you can build it into a hillside, it will be easier to clean. Think "walkout basement" style house where the walkout part of the basement provides a way to rake the pit out for cleaning.
2. Dig a hole. For a 1 seat outhouse, you need a hole that is roughly 4x4x5.
3. Start the foundation by reinforcing the walls of the hole with pressure treated wood or regular wood wrapped in tar paper. If you don't have these supplies, you can use sheet plastic or anything else that will help keep the wood from getting too wet.
4. Build a base for the floor. A simple square or rectangle made from 4x4s of pressure treated wood will work.

5. Use plywood to create the floor. Cut a hole where the seat will be and attach the "floor" to the foundation for stability.
6. Build the seat. 1.5 feet high is generally a good height.
7. Frame the outside and cover with a roof.
8. Make sure there is ventilation from the pit to the outside but that flies cannot get into the pit.

To manage the contents of the pit, toss a cup full of wood ash in the hole after each use. An outhouse of this size needs to be raked out about once a month if it is being used by two people. The contents can be buried or, if broken down sufficiently can be used as fertilizer on pasture or fields.

Bathing

The first realization you will need to accept is that you are not going to be as clean as you are used to being when you do not have access to modern plumbing for an extended period of time. However, bathing and hand washing are important to maintaining the level of hygiene that will keep your family healthy. The primary obstacle to bathing without power is access to water. Fortunately, you can bathe in water that you would not want to drink which gives you more options.

- You can use a local water source like a river or lake for bathing. However, this water will be very cold and if you are using it as a primary water source, you risk contaminating it with soap and shampoo.
- Water can be collected from a river, lake, or even a rainstorm and used for filling bathtubs and for sponge bathing. This is how our ancestors bathed before they had indoor plumbing. This method requires work as you will have to haul the water from

wherever it is to wherever you will be bathing, but if you have the resources to heat it first, you could even have a warm bath.

- You can also use specific kinds of shampoo and body soap that are meant to be used with very little or even no water. These products, which are usually used to bathe convalescent people, can generally be found online. You also have the option of making your own dry shampoo with a few simple ingredients. Here is a simple recipe for dry shampoo.

Combine ¼ cup of cornstarch and 1 tablespoon of baking soda in a small airtight container. Shake to mix.

To use this shampoo, shake a small amount into your hand, work it into your hair, brush through, and you are done.

Hand Washing

Maintaining a strict regimen of hand washing is going to be crucial to maintaining safe sanitary conditions. Most of us wash our hands several times a day but when access to running water is limited and your activities shift from work and leisure to survival, you will need to wash your hands on a more frequent basis. At a minimum, hands should be washed

- Before eating and going to sleep
- Before and after preparing or handling food, caring for someone who is injured or ill, and administering first aid of any kind
- After using the bathroom, coughing, sneezing, or blowing your nose
- After coming into contact with anyone else's hands, changing a diaper, taking out garbage, or handling animals

Potable water should be used for hand washing.

Dishes

Unfortunately, there is no dishwasher if there is no electricity but it is important to maintain sanitary plates, glasses, and utensils for your family to use for eating. You may think that stocking some paper plates and plastic forks may be the answer, but using disposable products causes other problems, especially over the long term. This means you are going to be washing dishes by hand. Thankfully, you aren't likely to need anything you don't already have on hand in order to wash the dishes. You will need to heat potable water to use for washing and rinsing dishes. Use the hottest water you can stand for the best possible result.

Trash

One of the reasons you should forgo the convenience of disposable tableware is that without power, trash collection services are unlikely to continue in the short or long term. This means you will need to deal with any trash your family creates which means the less trash, the better. Generally speaking, a family of 4 in this country produces about 4 pounds of trash each day. That means you will have more than 50 pounds of trash to deal after the first week with no trash pickup.

Your first job is to reduce that amount however you can. The easiest way to do this is start thinking about everything that goes in your trash can to determine if it can be disposed of some other way. For example, any kitchen scraps should be used to start a composting pile. Any paper or cardboard should be set aside to be burnt and anything that can be recycled, repurposed, or reused, should be cleaned, sanitized, and set aside or put to use.

Next, you need to deal with whatever is left. The best option is to bury it. This will keep it from attracting animals and eliminate the odor that can quickly accumulate when garbage is piled up and just sits. Make sure you choose a location to bury your trash that is 200 feet and down slope from your water source and remove the trash from the plastic bags before burying it to hasten the degradation of anything that can decompose.

What to Do Now to be Ready

- Add the supplies necessary to create a temporary toilet to your preps.
- Identify possible locations for building a temporary latrine or more permanent outhouse. This is especially important if you live in an urban or suburban setting.
- Research and design the outhouse you would build if necessary and purchase any specific supplies you would need to construct it.
- Add shampoo and soap to your preps that will enable you to bathe with minimal amounts of water.
- Consider adding a large tub that can be used for bathing to your preps.
- Make sure you have enough hand soap and dish soap on hand to last for several months.
- Start reducing the amount of trash you produce now by composting, reusing, repurposing, and recycling as much as possible.

Cooking, Heating, Cooling, Lighting

We often forget how much easier are lives are than the lives lived by our great grandparents and their families. The modern home is a wonder filled with appliances and equipment that make our lives easier and more comfortable. Unfortunately, most of these amenities will not work without electricity which means we need to be ready to survive without them if the grid goes down.

Feeding Your Family

The greatest immediate food-related loss in a grid down situation will be your refrigerator. Perishable food items must be kept below 41°F to remain safe. Most refrigerators will be able to maintain that temperature for about 4-8 hours without electricity as long as they are opened infrequently. Food kept in a freezer can remain viable for 1-2 days if the freezer is full and access is limited. But, as soon as the temperature rises above that threshold, the food in the refrigerator or the freezer has to be discarded.

If your local climate includes winters were the average temperature is lower than 41°F, power outages that occur during these months may allow you to use a cooler and the outside temperature to maintain perishable items. However, you will need a thermometer to track the temperature in whatever location you choose to use to store perishables so that you will know when food is no longer safe to eat. Once the food in the refrigerator and freezer is no longer viable, you need to dispose of it. Do not leave it in the refrigerator to rot as this can create unsanitary conditions inside your home.

As you will not be able to count on grocery stores and other shops to be open or have products for sale, you will need to have a supply of non-perishable items on hand to feed your family. As with water, you need to use your best judgment to determine how much food you want to store in preparation for an emergency. Most families need to balance space and budget against the possibility of a crisis to find the amount of non-perishable food items that offer peace of mind. Keep in mind, however, that unlike water, which must be treated but can generally be found after a power outage, you may only have access to the amount of food you have on hand at the time of the outage for the foreseeable future.

In order to address long term food needs, you may want to consider developing skills like gardening, raising livestock, hunting, fishing, trapping, and butchering that will enable you to produce a more sustainable food supply for your family in long term grid down situations.

Cooking the food that you have may also present some challenges as most cooking appliances require electricity. You may already have options available to you like a gas or charcoal grill, a wood stove or fireplace, or a camp stove. However, as each of these options requires some kind of fuel, you need to carefully consider what you can use for cooking and heating water in both the short and long term. While most preppers feel that more options are better, you may want to consider sticking with two, one that is short term like a gas grill with a few extra propane canisters and one that is long term like a wood burning stove plus a solar oven.

The most important thing to remember when it comes to cooking with these alternative methods is that you must not use grills, camp stoves, or other temporary heat producing sources inside the house as you risk carbon monoxide poisoning and other problems. Unless you are using something like a stove or a woodstove that is permanently installed inside your house, keep your cooking activities outside.

Maintaining a Healthy Environment

The next most pressing need is shelter. In a grid down scenario, you should be able to remain in your home as damage caused by other disasters is unlikely to have rendered it uninhabitable. This means you have a safe shelter. However, that shelter will only be safe if you can keep it warm or cool enough to maintain the health of your family members. If the outage occurs in the winter months, the furnace you rely on for heat will not operate without electricity. In order to remain in the safety of your home, you will need an alternative way to provide the heat needed to protect your family's health.

Unfortunately, as history has shown us, one of the first things people do when confronted with these problems is also one of the worst things they can do. They bring heat sources like grills, hibachis, and even fire pits that are meant to be used outside, inside without realizing that they are creating an environment that will kill them much more quickly than the cold. In fact, the majority of deaths that occur during cold weather power outages result from carbon monoxide poisoning, not from hypothermia.

The best way to ensure you will be able to keep your family warm if the grid is down in the winter is to invest in safe indoor heating sources that do not require electricity. This can include things like a wood stove, fireplace, or kerosene heater. Planning for how to handle this dire situation now will make it possible for you to have the things you will need in place if you are without power for an extended period of time.

Cold weather has to be the top priority for anyone who lives in states that experience low temperatures, but that doesn't mean people in states where the weather gets hot have it easy. Heat can be just as deadly as cold if not managed properly and when the grid goes down, there will be no access to air conditioning to provide safe sanctuary from the heat.

Unfortunately, there aren't any good, quick solutions to keeping things cool without electricity. If the power goes out in the summer months, you will need to make adjustments to your routine in order to protect yourself from overheating. This can mean changing your schedule around to that you are getting up very early to take care of chores that are labor intensive, resting during the hottest parts of the day, and resuming activity in the evening. If you live somewhere that it is feasible to have a basement or cellar, you may consider putting one in or finishing the one that you have for when the temperature soars. Because of their underground location, these areas will remain cooler than the rest of the house even on the hottest days.

Lighting the Night

It won't take very many days without power for you to understand why our ancestors got up with the sun and went to bed shortly after it did. While having dinner by candlelight might be romantic from time to time, cooking, working, cleaning, and doing most other things in this kind of low light atmosphere is generally more challenging than we expect it will be. And this assumes that we have enough candles or other sources of illumination on hand when the power goes out to provide the light we need to perform these tasks in a world that is much darker than we realize, once all the electrical lights are gone.

Candles can be used safely in some circumstances but they do increase the risk of fire which is why oil lamps and lanterns that use a contained flame are a better long term solution for grid down lighting. As this is something you are not likely to have on hand, it is definitely something you need to purchase as part of your preparedness efforts. Make sure you have enough lamps, oil, and wicks to provide the light your family needs to navigate safely in the dark for an extended timeframe.

If you don't have premade lamps on hand, you can build your own with a few things you are likely to have around the house. You will need:

- A wide mouth glass jar
- A wick
- A length of steel wire
- Olive oil or other vegetable based oil

Twist one end of the wire in a coil around the wick so that a ¼ inch of the wick is protruding from one side of the coil and the long tail of the wick from the other. Bend the wire so that it makes a "J" shape , the end with the wick attached should be at the top of the short side. Measure out the wire so that the bottom of the "J" rests on the bottom of the jar and the other end of the wire hooks over the edge of the jar. Pull out the wire and add olive oil or other vegetable oil to the bottom. You want enough olive oil to reach just below where the wire is twisted around the wick. Put the wire/wick in the jar and light the wick. A few ounces of oil will last for several hours. As the wick burns, you may need to pull more wick through the wire coil.

What to Do Now to Be Ready

- Purchase a thermometer for use in your refrigerator and freezer so you can monitor the interior temperature during a power outage.
- Determine how much non-perishable, shelf-stable food you want to store for use in emergency situations based on your family size and begin building a stockpile to meet those needs.
- Develop skills that can help you provide food for your family like gardening, raising livestock, hunting, fishing, trapping, and butchering.
- Consider starting a garden or raising chickens to establish some food independence and sustainability.
- Invest in at least two alternative methods for cooking that can be conducted without electricity.
- Learn to cook using these methods now so that you don't waste precious food supplies later.
- Invest in alternative sources of heat that do not require electricity like a wood stove or kerosene heater
- Consider putting in a basement or cellar or finishing off one you already have to provide a cooler environment during hot days.
- Stock up on oil lamps and lanterns, lamp oil, wicks, and hand crank flashlights to provide lighting.

Conclusion

The threat of an extended power outage or a grid down scenario is real and if it is realized, it will bring our modern world to a standstill. Water won't be pumped into homes, trucks won't be able to deliver food to stores, and people will huddle together shivering in their cold, dark homes.

Looters will roam the streets and desperate people will begin doing desperate things just to survive. You will need a strategy to deal with this aspect of life after the grid goes down as well. For more information on what you can do to defend your home and your family, read "*The Hunkering Down Guide to Protect and Defend Your Home When Disaster Strikes*" and "*Prepping for Violence: The Self Defense Guide to Protect and Defend Your Family When Society Collapses*", from the "*Survival Family Basics*" series.

Make sure you and your family have the knowledge, skills, and supplies needed to survive and thrive in a world without power by taking the time to understand the implications of a long term power outage and then creating a plan for how to handle things like sanitation and food preparation without the modern tools we are accustomed to using.

Thinking through scenarios and considering the available options will help you decide what skills you need to develop and supplies you need to have on hand to take care of the following without electricity after the grid goes down:

- Find, treat, and store enough water to meet your family's needs
- Manage hygiene and sanitation without running water
- Handle human waste safely
- Follow proper hygiene practices to keep hands, bodies, dishes, and other food preparation utensils clean

- Manage the trash your family produces when pickup stops
- Keep your family safe and warm during the winter months
- Cook meals safely
- Provide a safe way to light your life

By reviewing the information provided here, you will have the information you need to develop your own plan for surviving in the initial aftermath of a large scale power outage and thriving over the long term.

From identifying how to heat your home without power to determining how much food you need to stockpile, this book encourages you to think about what you need to know, do, and have in order to keep your family safe and healthy when the grid goes down.

Happy Prepping!

Macenzie

Check out these other *Survival Family Basics* Titles...

http://www.amazon.com/dp/B00HG7Y4YS

http://www.amazon.com/dp/B00HYQ55W6

http://www.amazon.com/dp/B00J1V939S

http://www.amazon.com/dp/B00I90UPSK

http://www.amazon.com/dp/B00JXU7OBG